The MAILBOX®

The Education Center®

Everything PreK-K

Nursery Rhymes

Timesaving tools for important skills practice

- Illustrated nursery rhymes
- Literacy and math practice
- Booklet-making ideas
- Fine-motor fun

- Quick crafts
- Games

Activities for 20 nursery rhymes!

Managing Editor: Kelly Robertson

Editorial Team: Becky S. Andrews, Diane Badden, Kimberley Bruck, Karen A. Brudnak, Pam Crane, Pierce Foster, Ada Goren, Tazmen Hansen, Marsha Heim, Lori Z. Henry, Debra Liverman, Kitty Lowrance, Brenda Miner, Jennifer Nunn, Tina Petersen, Mark Rainey, Greg D. Rieves, Hope Rodgers, Eliseo De Jesus Santos II, Rebecca Saunders, Donna K. Teal, Rachael Traylor, Sharon M. Tresino

www.themailbox.com

©2010 The Mailbox® Books
All rights reserved.
ISBN10 #1-56234-932-5 • ISBN13 #978-1-56234-932-5

Withdrawn

Mary Had a Little Lamb

Mary had a little lamb.
Its fleece was white as snow.
And everywhere that Mary went
The lamb was sure to go.
It followed her to school one day,
Which was against the rule.
It made the children laugh and play
To see a lamb at school.

Everything Nursery Rhymes • ©The Mailbox® Books • TEC61259

Humpty Dumpty

Humpty Dumpty sat on a wall.
Humpty Dumpty had a great fall.
All the king's horses
And all the king's men
Couldn't put Humpty together again.

What's

illustrated nursery rhymes

...ctice pages

Name

Cross out...

Name

Busy Little Pigs

Trace.

Everything Nursery Rhymes • ©The Mailbox® Books • TEC61259

"Twinkle, Twinkle, Little Star"

Matching numbers to sets

Counting Stars

...h the numbers to the sets.

Everything Nursery Rhymes • ©The Mailbox® Books • TEC61259

3 5 9 10

Inside

multipurpose picture cards

class booklet activities

Plus more ways to use the teaching tools!

quick crafts

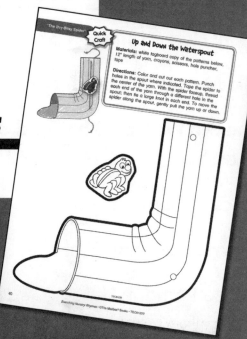

Table of Contents

Bowwow

"Bowwow," says the dog.
"Mew, mew," says the cat.
"Grunt, grunt," says the hog,
And "squeak" goes the rat.

"Buzz, buzz," says the bee.
"Caw, caw," says the crow.
"Quack, quack," says the duck.
And what the cuckoo bird says, you know!

"Bowwow" Picture Cards

TEC61259

TEC61259

TEC61259

TEC61259

TEC61259

TEC61259

TEC61259

TEC61259

Everything Nursery Rhymes • ©The Mailbox® Books • TEC61259

Class Book Cover: Have each child draw a self-portrait on a blank sheet of paper. Next, ask him to choose a real or made-up word he likes to say. On his paper, write the following sentence: "[Word, word]!" says [student's name]. Then stack the pages behind a construction paper copy of this cover and staple them together.

Quick Craft

Cuckoo Clock

Materials: craft feathers (optional), 9" construction paper square, 1" x 6" construction paper strip, construction paper scraps, scissors, glue, crayons

Directions: Color the clock. Cut out the three patterns and glue them on the paper square. Accordion-fold the paper strip and glue one end to the clock where indicated. To make a cuckoo bird, tear from the paper scraps two different-size circles, two wing shapes, and a small triangle (beak). Color two eyes on the smaller circle (head) and then glue the beak in place. Glue the head and wing shapes to the larger circle (body). Add craft feathers and glue the bird to the unattached end of the paper strip.

Glue here.

Cuckoo!

Cuckoo!

TEC61259

Name _____

Dog and Hog

✂ Cut.

📎 Glue to match the rhyming pictures.

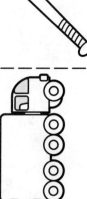

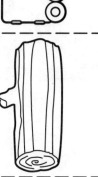

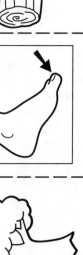

Everything Nursery Rhymes • ©The Mailbox® Books • TEC61259

9 **Note to the teacher:** Before instructing students to complete the page, have them name each featured character from "Bowwow."

Name _____

Buzz, Buzz!

✏️ Color to show how many.

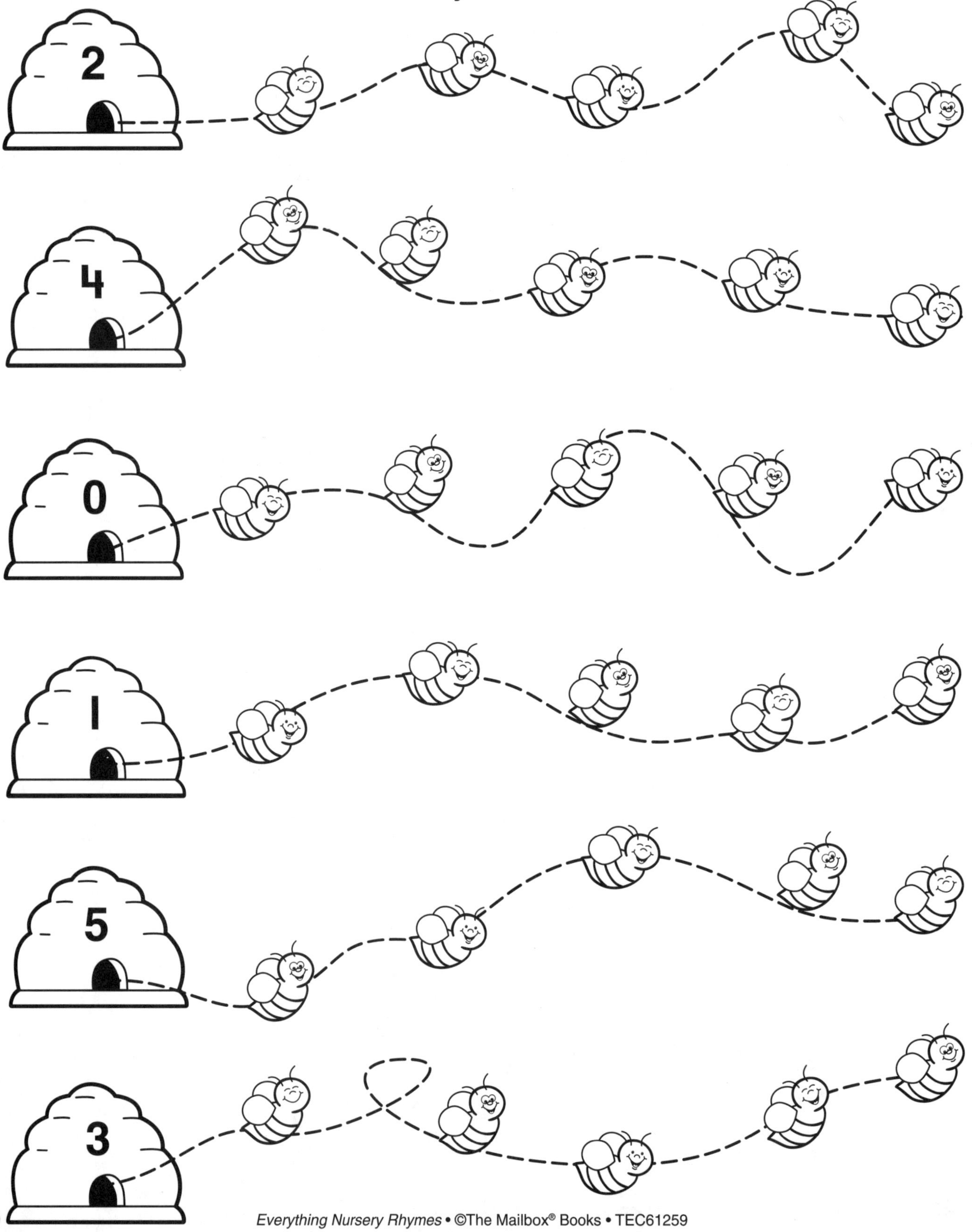

2

4

0

1

5

3

A Bunch of Talkers

Color.

Cut.

Glue.

Everything Nursery Rhymes • ©The Mailbox® Books • TEC61259

Note to the teacher: Each child needs a four-inch square of construction paper for fence posts. A child colors the artwork and cuts the construction paper square into strips. Next, he trims the strips as needed and glues them on the paper to finish the fence.

11

Name _____

Happy Hog

 Cut.

Glue to make a picture.

Everything Nursery Rhymes • ©The Mailbox® Books • TEC61259

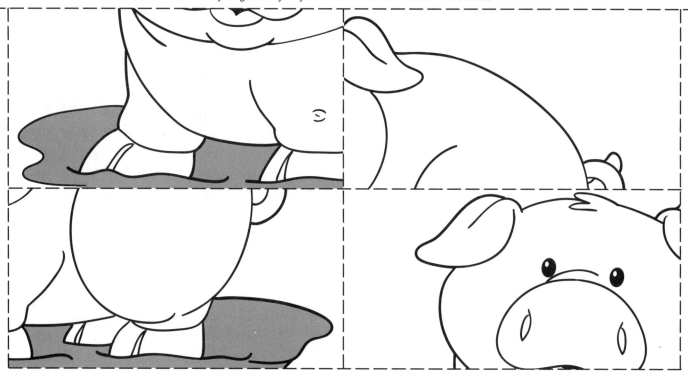

Hey, Diddle, Diddle

Hey, diddle, diddle,
The cat and the fiddle,
The cow jumped over the moon;
The little dog laughed
To see such fun,
And the dish ran away with the spoon.

TEC61259

TEC61259

TEC61259

TEC61259

TEC61259

TEC61259

What Makes Us Laugh?

Class Book Cover: Give each child a sheet of paper programmed with the prompt "I laugh when I…" If a child is not sure how to complete the prompt, give suggestions such as "read a silly book," "see Grandma without her teeth," or "hear my brother's burp!" Have her dictate or write a response and illustrate the page. Then stack the pages behind a construction paper copy of this cover and staple them together.

Quick Craft

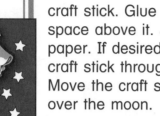

Over the Moon

Materials: 12" x 18" sheet of black construction paper, jumbo craft stick, tape, scissors, crayons, glue, foil star stickers (optional)

Directions: Color and cut out the patterns. Tape the cow to the craft stick. Glue the moon to the paper near the bottom, leaving space above it. Just above the moon, cut a six-inch slit in the paper. If desired, attach foil star stickers to the paper. Slide the craft stick through the slit so the cow sits just above the moon. Move the craft stick back and forth so the cow appears to jump over the moon.

TEC61259

TEC61259

Name _____

On the Move

Color the pictures with the same beginning sound in each row.

Name _____

Play It Again!

Color the pictures that are the same size.

Name

Let's Go!

Trace.

Crumple.

Glue.

Note to the teacher: Have students trace the dish and the spoon. Then have each child crumple six tissue paper squares and glue one to the top of each flower stem.

Name _____

Does It Belong?

Cross out 4 things that are not part of the rhyme.

Everything Nursery Rhymes • ©The Mailbox® Books • TEC61259

Hickory, Dickory, Dock

Hickory, dickory, dock,
The mouse ran up the clock.
The clock struck one;
The mouse ran down,
Hickory, dickory, dock.

"Hickory, Dickory, Dock" Picture Cards
Use the extra animal cards to make more "Hickory, Dickory, Dock" rhymes.

mouse

TEC61259

cat

TEC61259

lizard

TEC61259

gerbil

TEC61259

TEC61259

When the Clock Strikes One

Class Book Cover: Give each child a sheet of paper and have him draw himself doing what he would normally be doing at one o'clock. Invite him to dictate or write a sentence about his drawing. Then stack the pages behind a construction paper copy of this cover and staple them together.

Quick Craft

Mouse on the Move

Materials: white construction paper copy of the pattern below, 2" brown paper oval, 2 small brown paper semicircles (ears), small pink paper circle (nose), 2 small pom-poms (eyes), craft stick, length of brown yarn (tail), crayons, scissors, tape, glue

Directions: Color and cut out the clock. Cut a slit along the dotted line. To make the mouse, glue the eyes, ears, and nose to one end of the oval. Then tape the tail to the opposite end of the oval. Glue the completed mouse to one end of the craft stick. Slide the craft stick through the slit so the mouse sits on the clock. Move the craft stick up and down so the mouse appears to run up and down the clock.

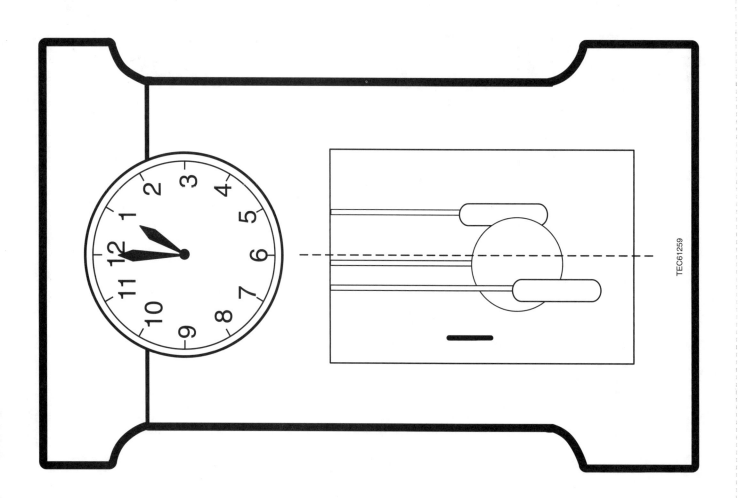

TEC61259

Name _____

Time to Climb

✂ Cut.

Glue to match the rhyming pictures.

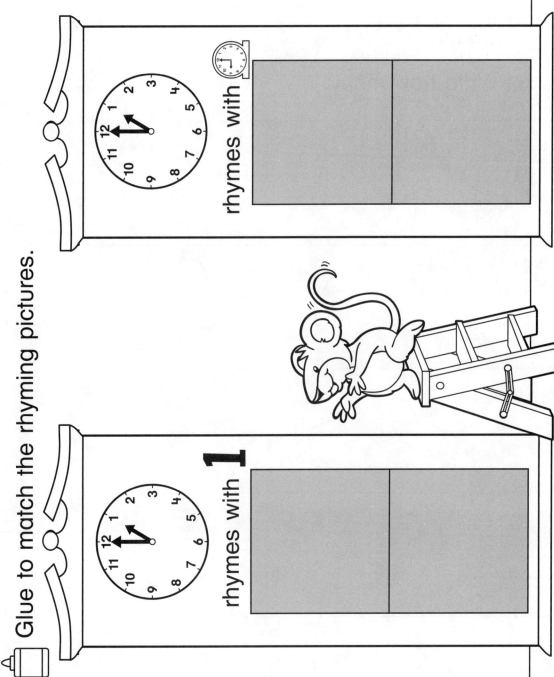

rhymes with

rhymes with **1**

Everything Nursery Rhymes • ©The Mailbox® Books • TEC61259

Name _____

Mouse Prints

"Hickory, Dickory, Dock"

Counting to ten

 Count.

Write how many.

Everything Nursery Rhymes •©The Mailbox® Books • TEC61259

To the Clock

Trace.

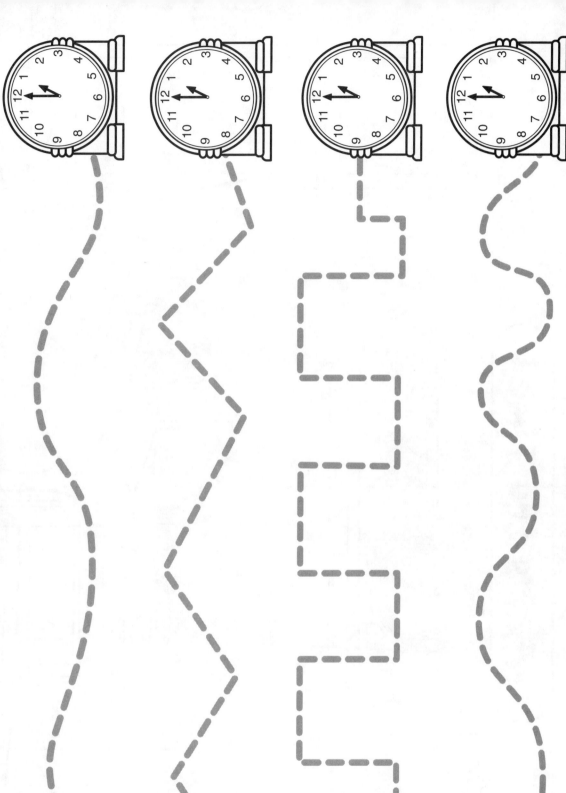

Name _____

What's the Time?

Color the 4 clocks.

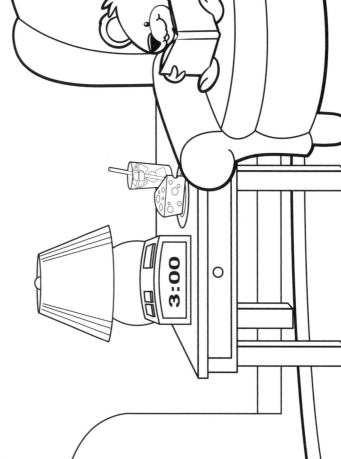

3:00

Humpty Dumpty

Humpty Dumpty sat on a wall.
Humpty Dumpty had a great fall.
All the king's horses
And all the king's men
Couldn't put Humpty together again.

"Humpty Dumpty" Picture Cards

Everything Nursery Rhymes • ©The Mailbox® Books • TEC61259

uh-Oh...
Something Fell!

Class Book Cover: Give each child a sheet of paper programmed with the prompt "One day, _____ fell…" Have him think of something that he heard or saw fall, such as a cup of milk, a book, or a friend. Have him dictate or write a response and illustrate the page. Then stack the pages behind a construction paper copy of this cover and staple them together.

Quick Craft

Humpty Dumpty's Wall

Materials: 9" x 12" sheet of light blue construction paper, red construction paper, crayons, scissors, glue

Directions: Color and cut out the pattern. Glue the pattern to the bottom of the paper (set horizontally). Then tear the red paper into rectangles (bricks) and glue them to the paper to complete the wall. Add desired details.

TEC61259

A Big Fall

Cut.

Glue the pictures in order.

1	2	3

Everything Nursery Rhymes • ©The Mailbox® Books • TEC61259

Name _____

A Great View!

Cut.
Glue.

  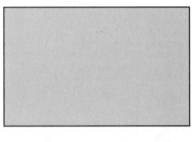

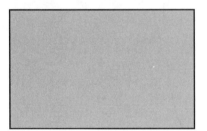  

Everything Nursery Rhymes • ©The Mailbox® Books • TEC61259

Note to the teacher: Help a child cut out the brick cards at the bottom of the page. Have him count the bricks and then count the rectangles

34   on the wall. Then have him glue each brick to a rectangle to match one to one.

Name _____

A Happy Hello!

Trace.

Color.

Name _____

Together Again

 Cut.

Glue to make a picture.

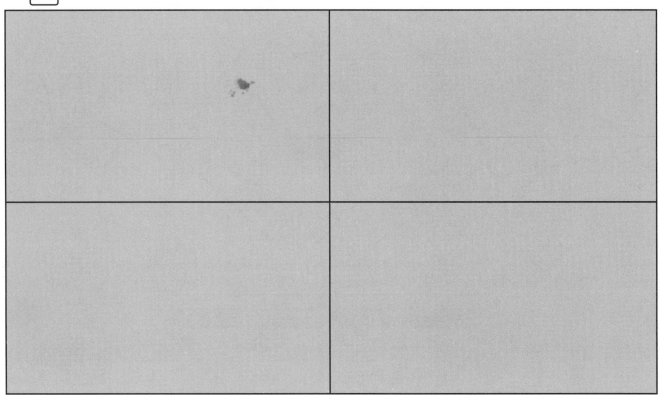

Everything Nursery Rhymes • ©The Mailbox® Books • TEC61259

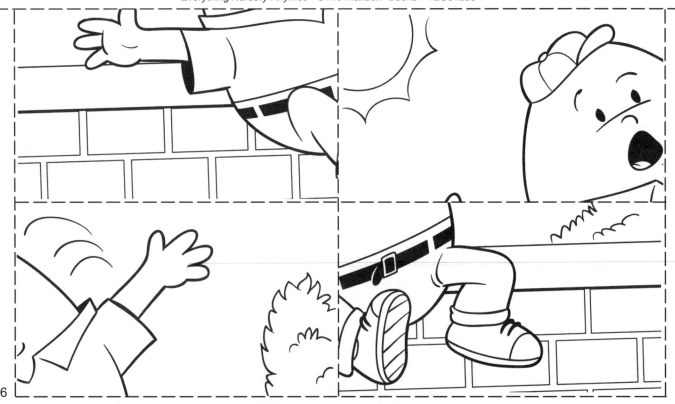

The Itsy-Bitsy Spider

The itsy-bitsy spider
Climbed up the waterspout.
Down came the rain
And washed the spider out.
Out came the sun
And dried up all the rain,
And the itsy-bitsy spider
Climbed up the spout again.

"The Itsy-Bitsy Spider" Picture Cards
Use the ladybug card for a different version of the rhyme.

TEC61259

TEC61259

TEC61259

TEC61259

TEC61259

TEC61259

Everything Nursery Rhymes • ©The Mailbox® Books • TEC61259

What Is Falling From the Sky?

Class Book Cover: Give each child a sheet of paper programmed with the prompt "One day, _____ fell from the sky and…" Have her dictate or write a response and then illustrate the page. Then stack the pages behind a construction paper copy of this cover and staple them together.

Quick Craft

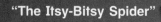

Up and Down the Waterspout

Materials: white tagboard copy of the patterns below, 12" length of yarn, crayons, scissors, hole puncher, tape

Directions: Color and cut out each pattern. Punch holes in the spout where indicated. Tape the spider to the center of the yarn. With the spider faceup, thread each end of the yarn through a different hole in the spout; then tie a large knot in each end. To move the spider along the spout, gently pull the yarn up or down.

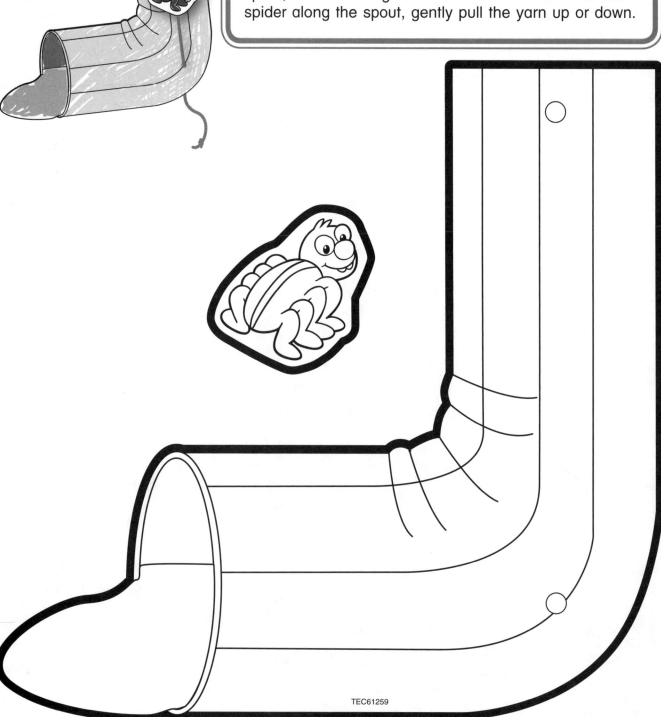

TEC61259

Up the Waterspout

✂ Cut. 🖊 Glue to match the letters.

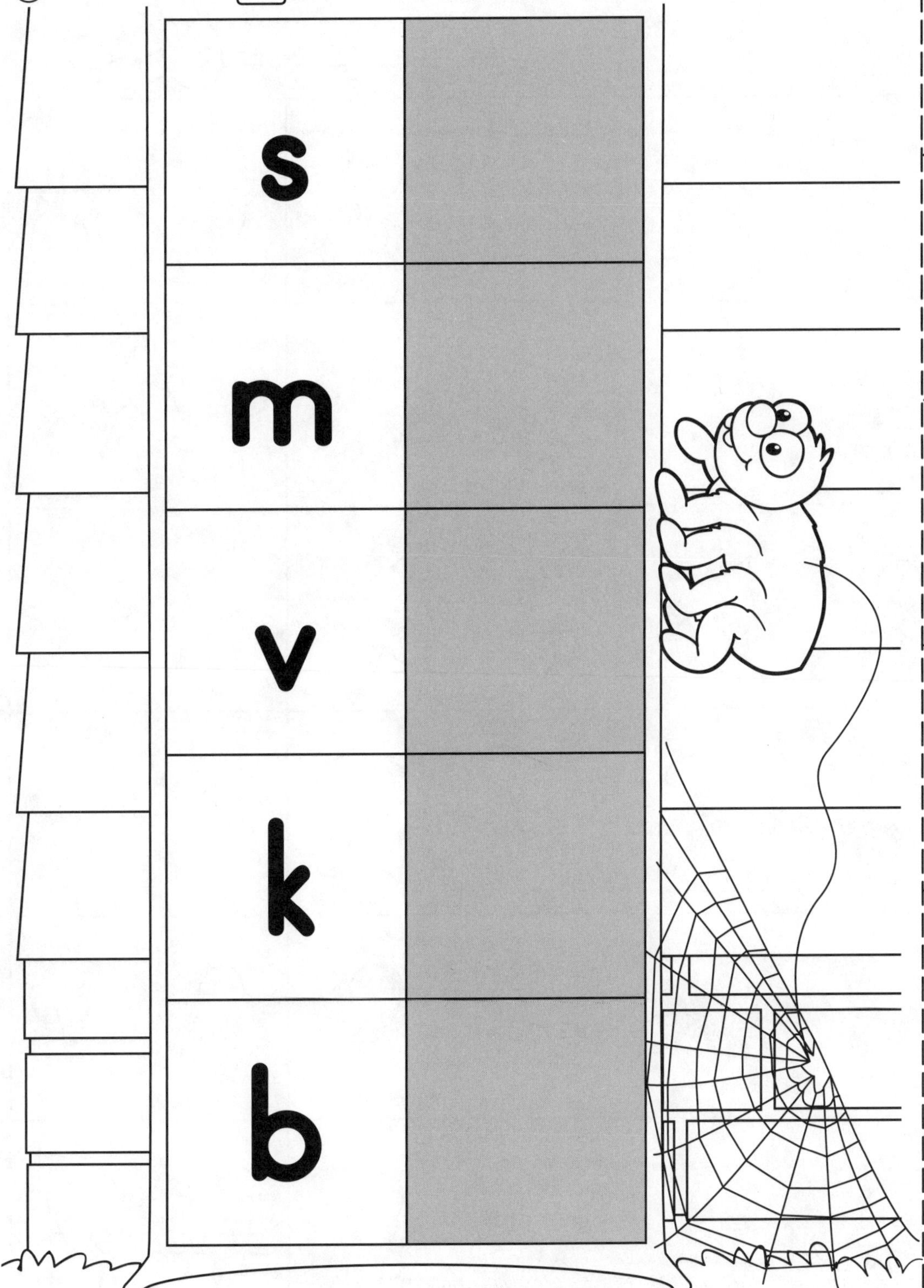

s	
m	
v	
k	
b	

b

v

s

k

m

Name _____

Rain or Shine?

AB pattern

What comes next?

Circle.

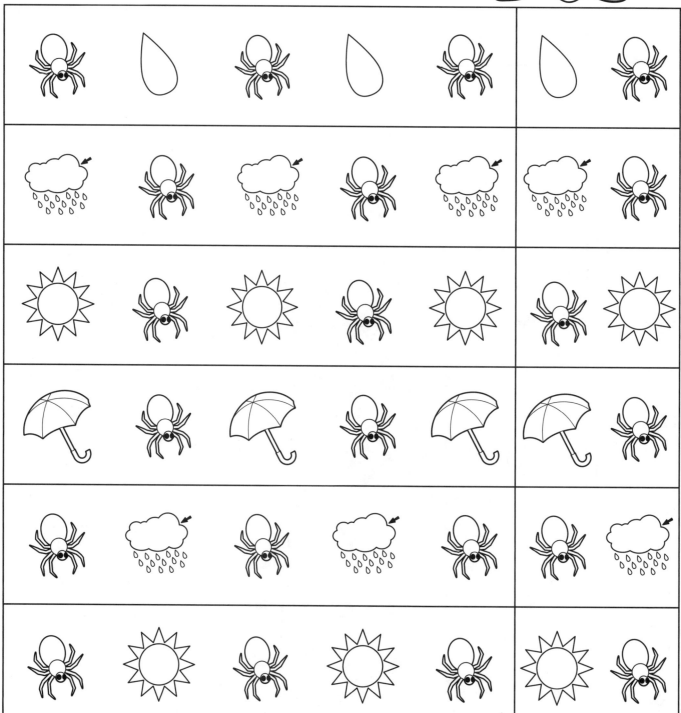

Name

Raindrops Are Falling

Color.

Tear.

Glue.

Everything Nursery Rhymes • ©The Mailbox® Books • TEC61259

Note to the teacher: After a child colors the page, have her tear blue construction paper scraps and glue them to the page so they look like raindrops.

Whee!

Connect the dots in order from 1 to 15.

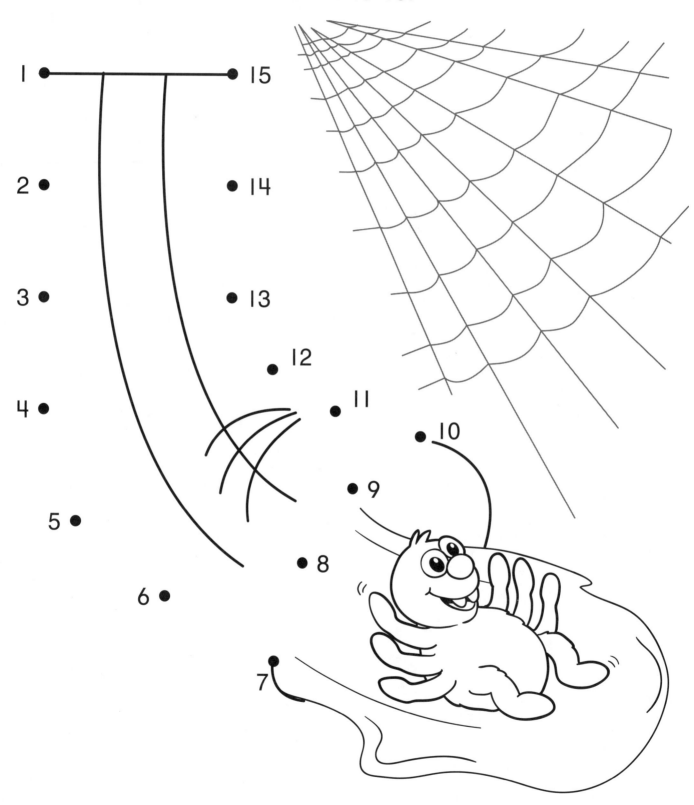

Jack and Jill

Jack and Jill went up the hill
To fetch a pail of water.
Jack fell down and broke his crown,
And Jill came tumbling after.

TEC61259

TEC61259

TEC61259

TEC61259

TEC61259

TEC61259

TEC61259

Everything Nursery Rhymes • ©The Mailbox® Books • TEC61259

What Can We Fetch?

Class Book Cover: Give each child a sheet of paper programmed with the sentence "I can fetch _____." Have him choose something he can fetch—such as his shoes, the mail, or a snack—and then dictate or write a response. Have him illustrate the page. Then stack the pages behind a construction paper copy of this cover and staple them together.

47

Quick Craft

Fancy Well

Materials: 9" white construction paper square, gray construction paper scraps, 1¼" piece of yarn, crayons, scissors, glue

Directions: Color the roof, posts, well handle, and pail. Cut out the pattern and glue it to the square. Tear the paper scraps and glue them to the bottom portion of the well. Then glue the yarn to the paper between the bottom of the roof and the handle of the pail.

TEC61259

Name _____

A Full Pail

🖍️ Color.

Everything Nursery Rhymes • ©The Mailbox® Books • TEC61259

Note to the teacher: Have a child name the first picture in each row and help her determine its beginning sound. Then have her color the three pictures in each row that have the same beginning sound.

49

Name _____

So Thirsty!

Cut.   Count.

Glue to match.

6   10   4   3   8

Name _____

At the Well

Trace.

Draw a 🪣.

Color.

52

Getting Some Water

Draw to help Jack and Jill find the well.

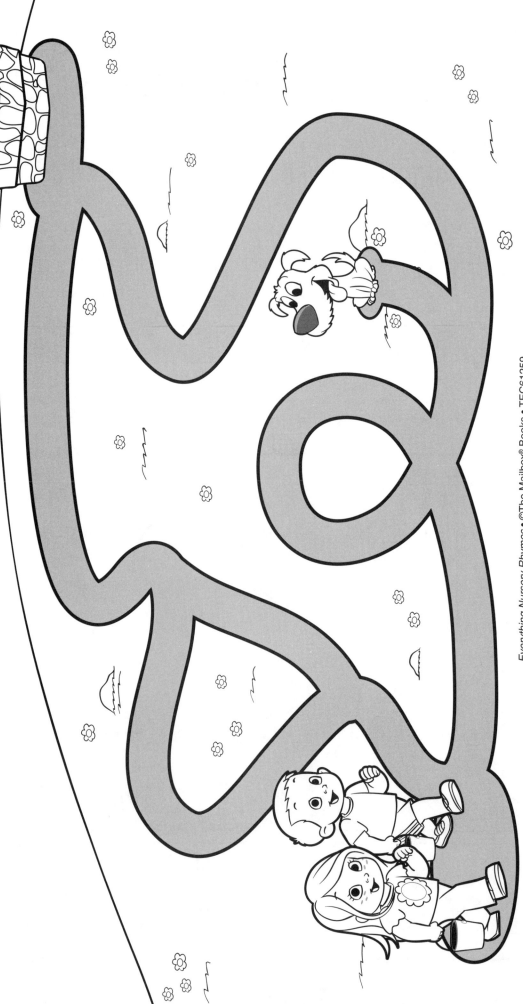

Little Bo Peep

Little Bo Peep has lost her sheep
And can't tell where to find them.
Just leave them alone,
And they'll come home
Wagging their tails behind them.

"Little Bo Peep" Picture Cards

Use the extra animal cards to make more "Little Bo Peep" rhymes.

Everything Nursery Rhymes • ©The Mailbox® Books • TEC61259

Lost and Found

Class Book Cover: Give each child a sheet of paper programmed with the prompt "One time I lost…" Have her dictate or write a response, naming an item she lost and telling where it was found. Have her illustrate the page. Then stack the pages behind a construction paper copy of this cover and staple them together.

Quick Craft

Finger Puppets

Materials: white construction paper copy of the patterns below, two 1" x 3" tagboard strips, tape, scissors, crayons or markers

Directions: Color and cut out the patterns; then laminate them for durability. From each tagboard strip make a loop and secure it with tape. Then tape a loop to the back of each cutout.

TEC61259

TEC61259

Lovely Letters

Circle the matching letters in each box.

M L L S L

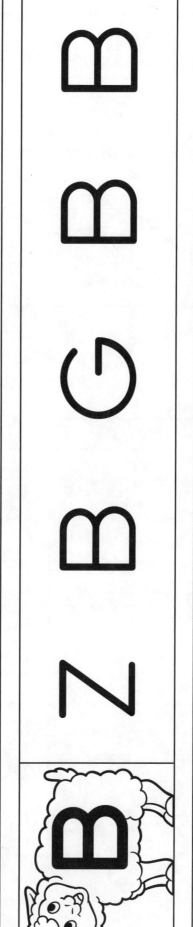

B B G Z B

P O P T P

Name _____

Welcome Home!

 Count.

Color each set that has **more**.

Woolly Sheep

Tear.

Crumple.

Glue.

Note to the teacher: Have a child tear and crumple small white tissue paper squares and glue them to each sheep so they resemble wool.

Name _____

60

Hide-and-Seek

Find 5 of Bo Peep's sheep.

✏️ Circle.

Little Boy Blue

Little Boy Blue,
Come blow your horn.
The sheep's in the meadow.
The cow's in the corn.
Where is the boy
Who looks after the sheep?
He's under a haystack,
Fast asleep.

"Little Boy Blue" Picture Cards

TEC61259

TEC61259

TEC61259

TEC61259

TEC61259

I Once Fell Asleep...

Class Book Cover: On a sheet of paper, have a child draw a strange place where he might fall asleep. Have him dictate or write a sentence about his drawing. Then stack the pages behind a construction paper copy of this cover and staple them together.

Quick Craft

Under the Haystack

Materials: 8" construction paper square, yellow construction paper scraps, scissors, glue, crayons, stapler

Directions: Color and cut out the Little Boy Blue pattern and glue it near the bottom of the paper square. Then tear the paper scraps into strips and glue the strips to the haystack pattern. Cut out the haystack pattern and place it on the paper square so it covers Little Boy Blue. Staple the haystack to the paper near the top.

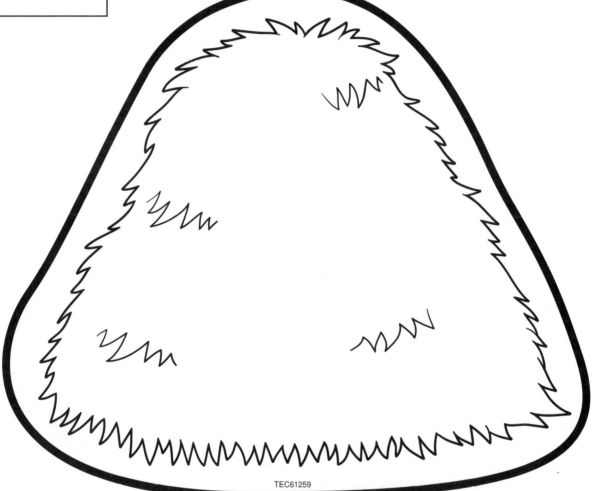

TEC61259

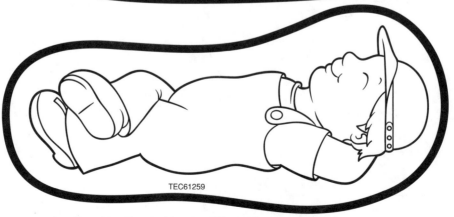

TEC61259

Name _____

Looking for Little Boy Blue

✂ Cut.

🧴 Glue to match the word families.

-an

-at

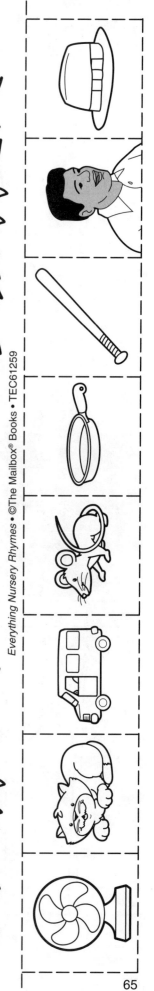

Eating Corn

✂ Cut.

Glue from the shortest to tallest.

Everything Nursery Rhymes • ©The Mailbox® Books • TEC61259

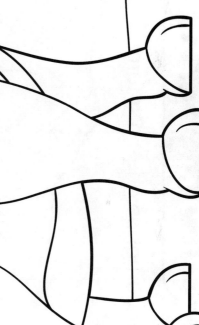

Name _____

Cow in the Corn

Color.

Tear.

Glue.

Everything Nursery Rhymes • ©The Mailbox® Books • TEC61259

Note to the teacher: After coloring the picture, have a child tear brown construction paper scraps and glue them to the cow so they look like spots.

67

Name _____

On the Farm

Circle 4 things that do not belong on a farm.

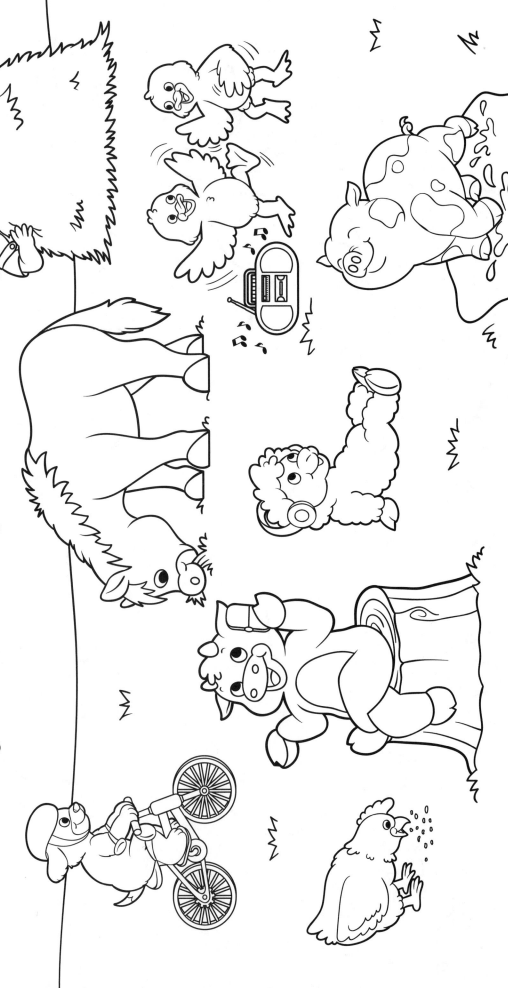

Little Jack Horner

Little Jack Horner
Sat in a corner
Eating his holiday pie.
He stuck in his thumb
And pulled out a plum
And said, "What a lucky boy am I!"

"Little Jack Horner" Picture Cards

Use the extra fruit cards to make more "Little Jack Horner" rhymes.

TEC61259

TEC61259

TEC61259

TEC61259

TEC61259

TEC61259

TEC61259

TEC61259

TEC61259

Our Favorite Pies

Everything Nursery Rhymes • ©The Mailbox® Books • TEC61259

Class Book Cover: On a blank sheet of paper, have each child draw herself eating a piece of her favorite pie. Next, have her dictate or write a sentence about her drawing. Then stack the pages behind a construction paper copy of this cover and staple them together.

Quick Craft

A Slice of Pie

Materials: 8" paper square, cotton ball, paint, sponges, crayons, scissors, glue

Directions: Sponge-paint the rectangular portion of the pie slice so it looks like a favorite flavor of pie. When the paint is dry, color the other parts of the pie slice. Then cut out the pie slice and the poem. Glue the cutouts to the paper square as shown. Then glue the cotton ball on the top of the pie slice so it looks like whipped cream.

Mmmm...Pie!

A big slice of pie
Is so good to eat.
Add some whipped cream
For a yummy treat.

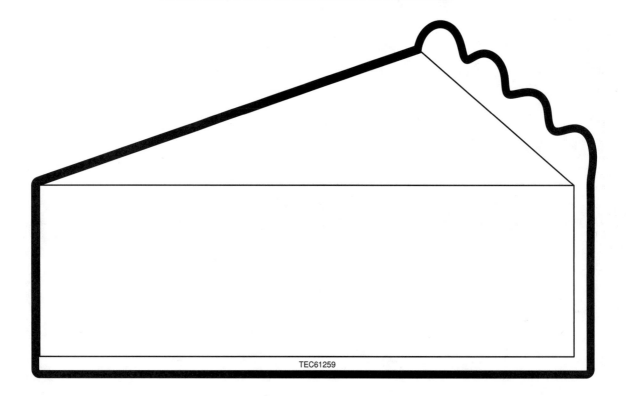

TEC61259

Ready for a Treat

✂ Cut.

⬜ Glue to match.

1	2	3

Everything Nursery Rhymes • ©The Mailbox® Books • TEC61259

Name

Cut. Sort.

Glue to match.

Plates of Pie

Everything Nursery Rhymes • ©The Mailbox® Books • TEC61259

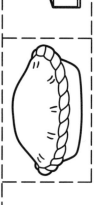

Adding a Crust

🖍 Color. ✂ Cut.

🧴 Glue.

Note to the teacher: Have each student color the pie to look like his favorite kind. Then have him cut a seven-inch brown paper square into strips. Encourage him to trim and glue the strips on the pie so they resemble a lattice crust.

Name _____

Trace.

Searching for Pie

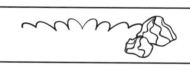

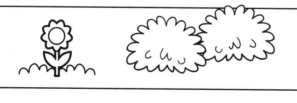

76

Little Miss Muffet

Little Miss Muffet
Sat on a tuffet,
Eating her curds and whey.
Along came a spider
That sat down beside her
And frightened Miss Muffet away.

"Little Miss Muffet" Picture Cards
Use the extra animal cards to make more "Little Miss Muffet" rhymes.

TEC61259

TEC61259

TEC61259

TEC61259

TEC61259

TEC61259

TEC61259

Everything Nursery Rhymes • ©The Mailbox® Books • TEC61259

Along Came a Spider!

Class Book Cover: Give each child a sheet of paper programmed with the prompt "I saw a spider _____, and I..." Encourage him to name where he saw a spider—such as crawling up a wall or in the bathtub—and dictate or write a response telling what he did when he saw it. Have him illustrate the page. Then stack the pages behind a construction paper copy of this cover and staple them together.

Quick Craft

Spider String Puppet

Materials: eight 6" construction paper strips, 12" length of yarn, jumbo craft stick, sharpened pencil, tape, crayons, scissors, glue

Directions: Color and cut out the spider pattern. Accordion-fold the paper strips (legs). Glue four legs to each side of the spider's body. Then tie one end of the yarn to the center of the craft stick. Use the pencil to poke a hole in the spider's body where indicated and thread the free end of the yarn through the hole. Tape the end of the yarn to the back of the spider. To make the spider move, manipulate the craft stick and yarn.

TEC61259

Everything Nursery Rhymes • ©The Mailbox® Books • TEC61259

Scared Away!

 Cut.

Glue the pictures in order.

1	2	3

Everything Nursery Rhymes • ©The Mailbox® Books • TEC61259

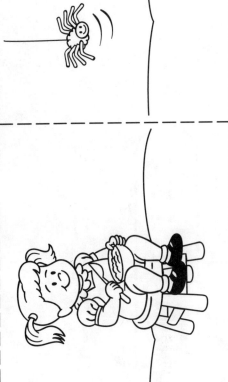

Name _____

Crawling Along

✂ Cut.

🧴 Glue to match one to one.

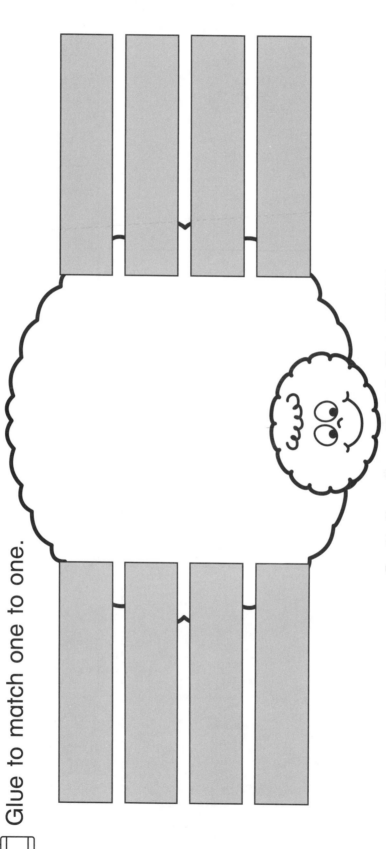

Everything Nursery Rhymes • ©The Mailbox® Books • TEC61259

Note to the teacher: Help a child cut out the cards at the bottom of the page. Have him count the spider legs and then count the number of boxes on each side of the spider. Then have him glue each leg to a box to match one to one.

Time to Go!

Trace.

Draw.

Color.

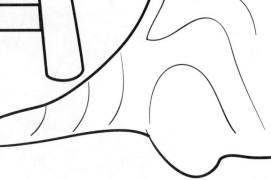

Note to the teacher: Have a child trace along the dotted lines. Then have her draw four legs on each side of the spider's body and a flower on each stem.

Name

84

Spider's Trail

✏️ Draw to help Spider find Miss Muffet.

Everything Nursery Rhymes • ©The Mailbox® Books • TEC61259

Mary Had a Little Lamb

Mary had a little lamb.
Its fleece was white as snow.
And everywhere that Mary went
The lamb was sure to go.
It followed her to school one day,
Which was against the rule.
It made the children laugh and play
To see a lamb at school.

SCHOOL

SCHOOL

HA! HA! HA!

School Rule
Leave lambs at home.

TEC61259

TEC61259

TEC61259

TEC61259

If Mary's Lamb Came to Our School...

Class Book Cover: Give each child a sheet of paper programmed with the prompt "If Mary's lamb came to our class, it could…" Have each student dictate or write something the lamb could do—such as sit by her at circle time, draw a picture for Mary, or eat a snack—and then illustrate her work. Stack the pages behind a construction paper copy of this cover and staple them together.

Quick Craft

Woolly Lamb

Materials: 6" tagboard circle, cotton balls, black crayon, scissors, glue

Directions: Draw facial features on the lamb's head and color the hooves. Cut out the patterns and glue them to the circle (body) as shown. Then gently pull apart the cotton balls and glue them to the top of the lamb's head and to the body.

TEC61259

Name _____

Learning Letters

Name each letter's sound.
Color the pictures that begin with the matching sound.

S

F

T

"Mary Had a Little Lamb"

Identifying beginning sounds

Everything Nursery Rhymes • ©The Mailbox® Books • TEC61259

89

Name _____

Little Lambs

Count.

Circle the set that has **fewer**.

Everything Nursery Rhymes • ©The Mailbox® Books • TEC61259

"Mary Had a Little Lamb"

Fine-motor skills

Lamb Goes to School

Trace.

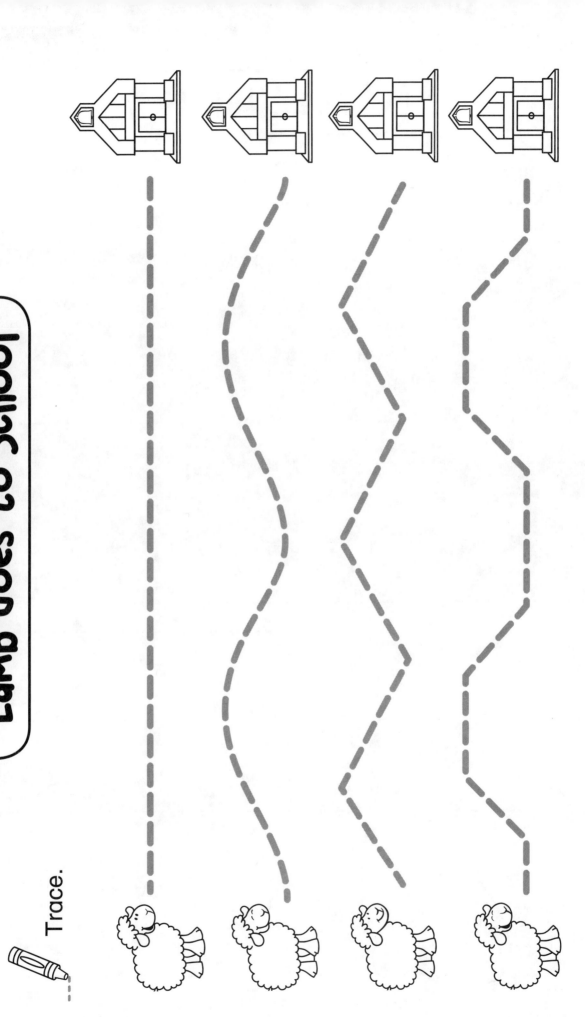

Everything Nursery Rhymes • ©The Mailbox® Books • TEC61259

Name _____

Sweet Lamb

✂ Cut.

🍼 Glue to make a picture.

Everything Nursery Rhymes • ©The Mailbox® Books • TEC61259

Old Mother Hubbard

Old Mother Hubbard
Went to the cupboard
To fetch her dog a bone;
But when she got there,
The cupboard was bare,
And so the poor dog had none.

"Old Mother Hubbard" Picture Cards

TEC61259

TEC61259

TEC61259

TEC61259

TEC61259

TEC61259

Everything Nursery Rhymes • ©The Mailbox® Books • TEC61259

What We Like to Eat!

Class Book Cover: Give each child a sheet of paper programmed with "[Child's name] likes to eat [name of food]." Have him dictate or write words to complete the sentence and draw a picture of himself eating the food. Then stack the pages behind a construction paper copy of this cover and staple them together.

Quick Craft

Filling Mother Hubbard's Cupboard

Materials: 9" paper square, grocery store circular or used magazine, crayons, scissors, glue

Directions: Color and cut out the cupboard pattern; then cut along the dotted lines. Glue the cupboard to the square, leaving the doors unattached. Next, cut from the circular or magazine several pictures of food items that would be appropriate to place in a cupboard. Then fold open the doors and glue the items inside the cupboard.

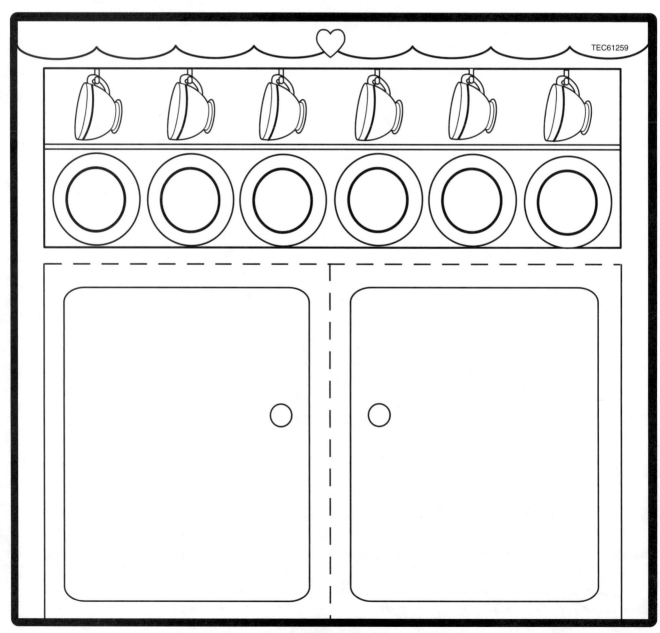

TEC61259

A Full Cupboard

Color 2 pictures in each row that rhyme.

Time to Eat!

Count.

✏ Circle to show how many.

Choices	Count	Bones
8 / 5		🦴🦴🦴🦴🦴
10 / 7		(10 bones)
11 / 15		(13 bones)
13 / 9		(11 bones)

Name

Yummy Bone

Trace.

Tear.

Glue.

Everything Nursery Rhymes • ©The Mailbox® Books • TEC61259

Note to the teacher: Have each child trace the bone. Then have her tear white tissue paper scraps and glue them to the bone.

Name _____

A Big Bowl

Connect the dots in order from 1 to 20.

Draw a 🦴 bone in the dish.

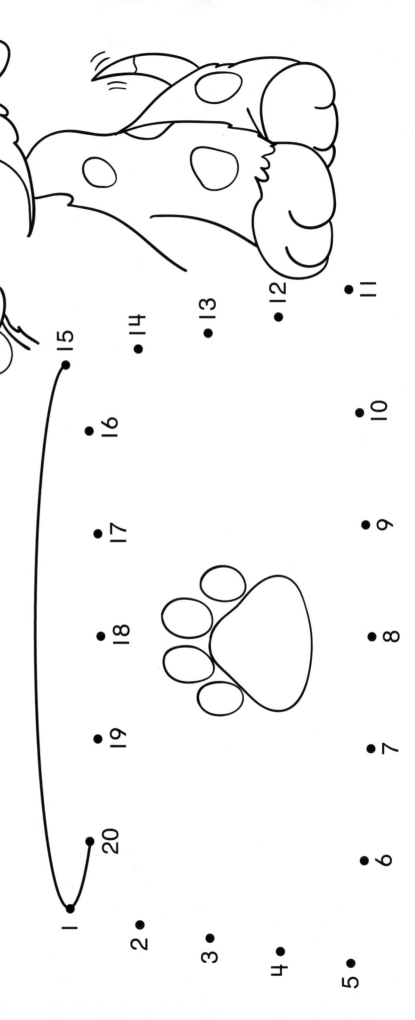

The Old Woman Who Lived in a Shoe

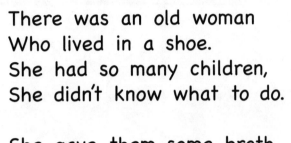

There was an old woman
Who lived in a shoe.
She had so many children,
She didn't know what to do.

She gave them some broth
And gave them some bread,
Then kissed them all soundly
And sent them to bed.

"The Old Woman Who Lived in a Shoe" Picture Cards

TEC61259

TEC61259

TEC61259

TEC61259

TEC61259

TEC61259

TEC61259

Everything Nursery Rhymes • ©The Mailbox® Books • TEC61259

Our Favorite Shoes

Class Book Cover: On a blank sheet of paper, have each child draw himself wearing a favorite pair of shoes. Have him dictate or write a sentence about his shoes. Then stack the pages behind a construction paper copy of this cover and staple them together.

Quick Craft

A House With Style

Materials: 9" x 12" sheet of construction paper, scissors, glue, crayons

Directions: Color and cut out the patterns. With your teacher's help, cut a door flap in the heel of the shoe, as shown. Then glue the shoe to the construction paper, being careful not to glue the door flap closed. Glue the window patterns to the shoe. Then glue the old woman to the picture and add other desired details.

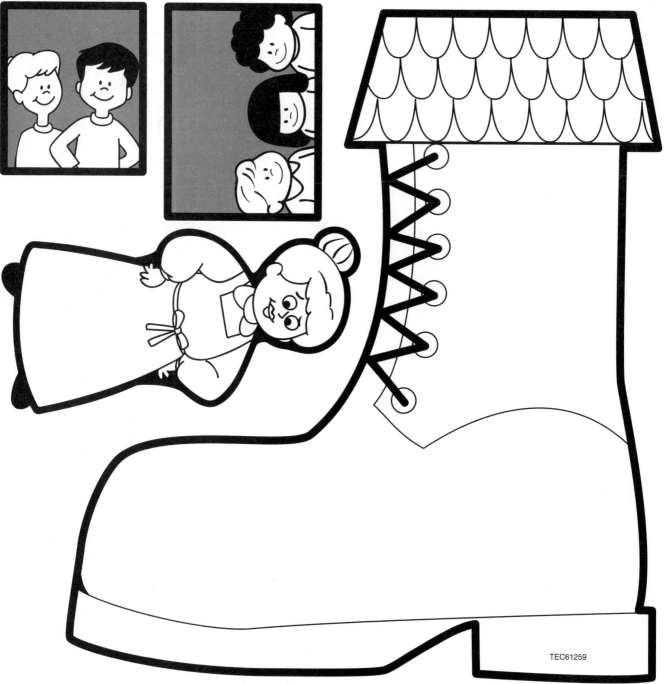

TEC61259

Time to Eat!

🖍 Color the bowls with matching letters.

Zz Dg

Mn Ff

Hh Qq Tf

Ij Ll Ww

Rr Kt Cc

Name _____

What comes next?

 Cut.

Glue.

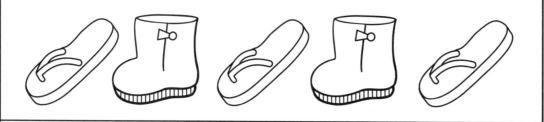

Everything Nursery Rhymes • ©The Mailbox® Books • TEC61259

Tucked In

Color.
Cut.
Glue.

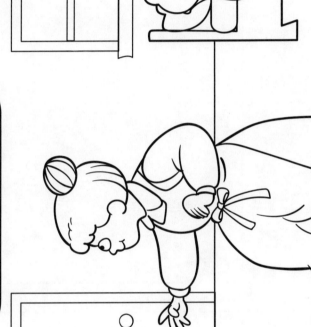

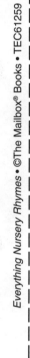

Everything Nursery Rhymes • ©The Mailbox® Books • TEC61259

Note to the teacher: Have each child color the picture. Then invite him to cut four rectangles (blankets) from construction paper scraps and glue one on each sleeping child in the picture.

Full House

Cut.

Glue to make a picture.

Once I Caught a Fish Alive

1, 2, 3, 4, 5.
Once I caught a fish alive.
6, 7, 8, 9, 10.
Then I let it go again.
Why did I let it go?
Because it bit my finger so.
Which finger did it bite?
The little one on the right.

"Once I Caught a Fish Alive" Picture Cards

Use the extra animal cards to make more "Once I Caught a Fish Alive" rhymes.

TEC61259

TEC61259

TEC61259

TEC61259

TEC61259

TEC61259

Everything Nursery Rhymes • ©The Mailbox® Books • TEC61259

1, 2, 3, 4, 5... What Would We Catch Alive?

Class Book Cover: Give each child a sheet of paper programmed with the prompt "1, 2, 3, 4, 5... I caught a _____ alive!" Have him dictate or write the name of a critter—such as a shark, a mouse, or a bear—and illustrate the page. Then stack the pages behind a construction paper copy of this cover and staple them together.

Quick Craft

Under the Sea

Materials: white construction paper copy of the pattern below, 12" x 18" sheet of light blue construction paper, scissors, glue, markers, spray bottle filled with water

Directions: Use markers to color the fish pattern. Cut out the fish and glue it to the construction paper. Draw underwater scenery on the paper using markers. Then generously spray the paper with water to give the picture an underwater effect.

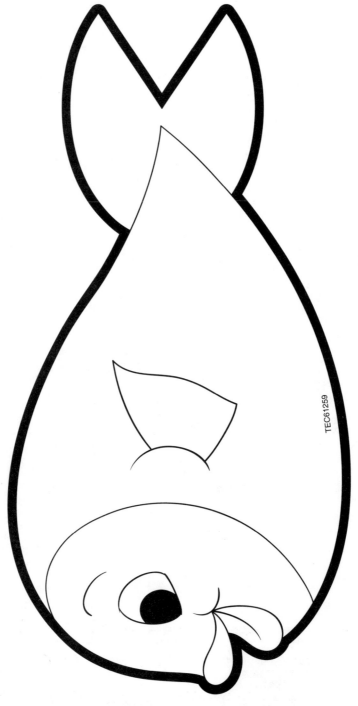

TEC61259

Name

"Once I Caught a Fish Alive"

Matching uppercase letters

Out of the Water

✂ Cut.

🍼 Glue to match the letters.

W	C

A	R

F	G

W   C   F

G   R   A

Everything Nursery Rhymes • ©The Mailbox® Books • TEC61259

113

Five Little Fish

Cut.

Glue the numbers in order.

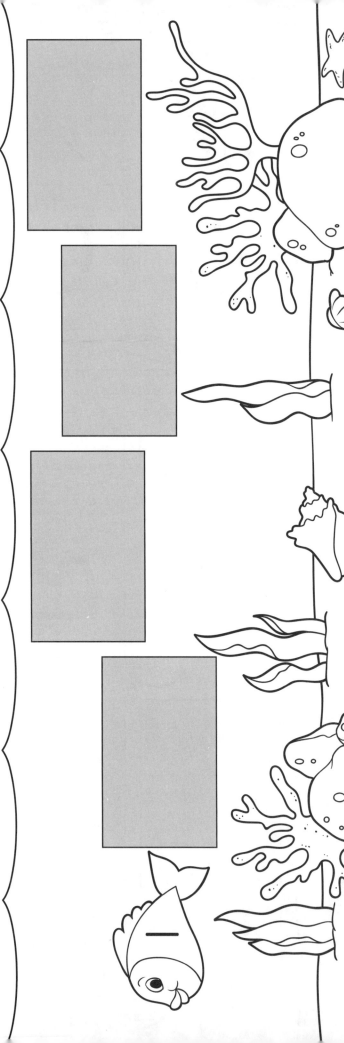

Everything Nursery Rhymes • ©The Mailbox® Books • TEC61259

Name

Fancy Fish

Draw to finish the fish.

Tear.

Glue.

Note to the teacher: Have each student finish the picture. Then have him tear tissue paper scraps (scales) and glue them to the fish.

115

Name _____

Fishing Fun

Cross off 4 things that do not belong

in this picture.

Everything Nursery Rhymes • ©The Mailbox® Books • TEC61259

Patty-Cake, Patty-Cake

Patty-cake, patty-cake, baker's man,
Bake me a cake as fast as you can.
Roll it and prick it and mark it with a *B*.
Put it in the oven for baby and me.

"Patty-Cake, Patty-Cake" Picture Cards

Use the extra cards to make more "Patty-Cake, Patty-Cake" rhymes.

TEC61259

TEC61259

TEC61259

TEC61259

TEC61259

TEC61259

TEC61259

TEC61259

Tasty Treats

Class Book Cover: On a sheet of paper, have each child draw his favorite baked good. Then encourage him to dictate or write a sentence about his drawing. Next, stack the pages behind a construction paper copy of this cover and staple them together.

Quick Craft

Decorate a Cake

Materials: 9" paper square, tissue paper squares, scissors, glue, crayons

Directions: Cut out the cake and glue it to the paper square. Crumple the tissue paper squares to make flowers and glue them to the cake. Then use crayons to add additional details to the cake as desired.

TEC61259

What to Buy?

Color the pictures in each row that start the same.

Name _____

So Many Treats

Count.

Write.

Everything Nursery Rhymes • ©The Mailbox® Books • TEC61259

What to write?

Trace.

Write.

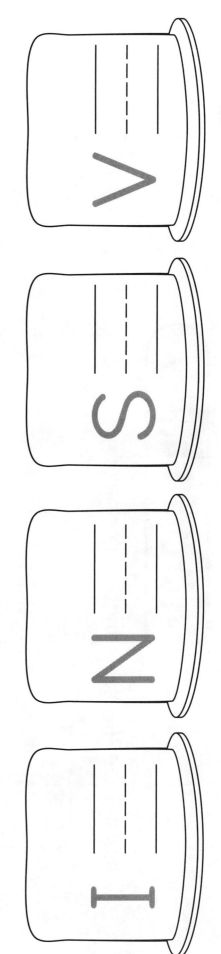

B

G

I

N

S

V

Name

At the Bakery

Cross out the 4 objects that do not belong.

124

Everything Nursery Rhymes • ©The Mailbox® Books • TEC61259

Pease Porridge Hot

Pease porridge hot,
Pease porridge cold,
Pease porridge in the pot
Nine days old.

Some like it hot.
Some like it cold.
Some like it in the pot
Nine days old.

hot

cold

Days

1	2	3	4	5	6	7
8	9					

What's in the Pot?

Class Book Cover: On a blank sheet of paper, have each child draw himself cooking something in a pot. Have him dictate or write a sentence about what is in his pot. Then stack the pages behind a construction paper copy of this cover and staple them together.

Quick Craft

Peas in a Pod

Materials: 9" x 12" white construction paper, green paint, sponge, green pipe cleaner, hole puncher, scissors, glue, crayons

Directions: Sponge-paint the construction paper. When the paint is dry, cut out several circles (peas). Then color and cut out the pea pod. Glue the peas to the pod. Then punch a hole in the pod and twist the green pipe cleaner through the hole as shown.

TEC61259

Name _____

Bowl of Peas

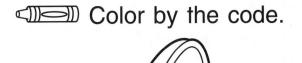 Color by the code.

Color Code

begins like 🍲 —green

begins like 🥜 —yellow

Name _____

130

✂ Cut. Measure.
✏ Write.

Sweet Peas

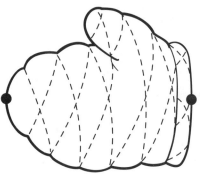

_____ peas

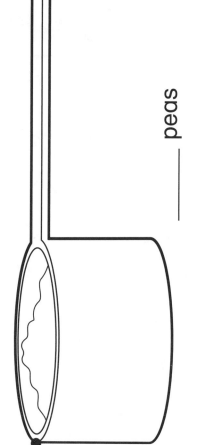

_____ peas

_____ peas

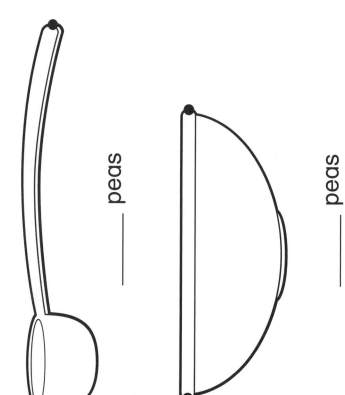

_____ peas

A Hot Pot

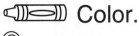 Color.

 Cut.

 Glue.

Everything Nursery Rhymes • ©The Mailbox® Books • TEC61259

Name _____

Eating Porridge

 Cut.

Glue to make a picture.

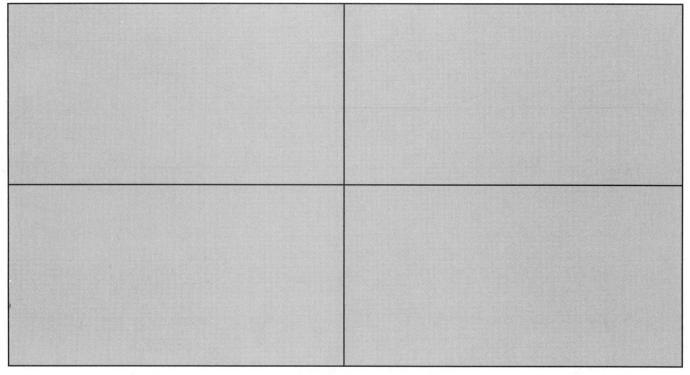

Everything Nursery Rhymes • ©The Mailbox® Books • TEC61259

Rub-a-Dub-Dub

Rub-a-dub-dub,
Three men in a tub,
And who do you think they be?
The butcher, the baker,
The candlestick maker,
And they all set out to sea.

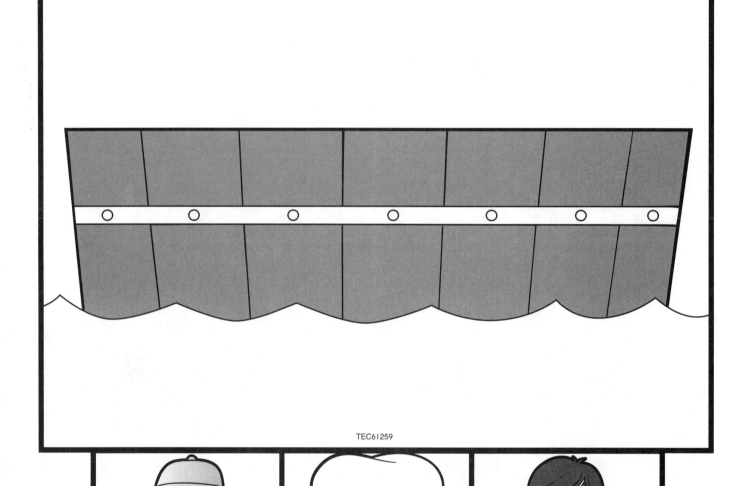

TEC61259

TEC61259

TEC61259

TEC61259

Who's in the Tub?

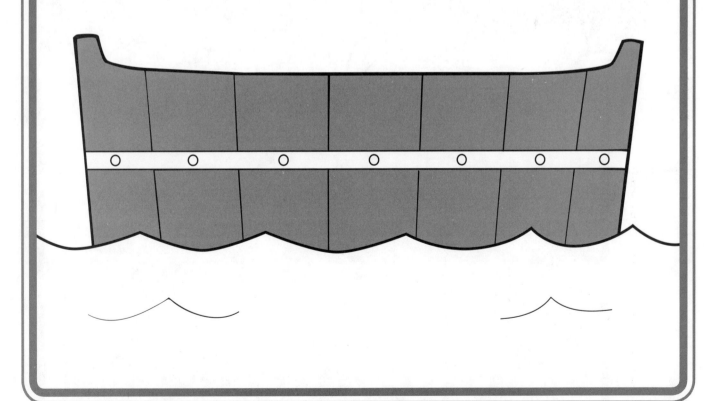

Class Book Cover: On a sheet of paper, have each child draw herself and two companions floating in a tub. Then have her dictate or write a sentence about her drawing. Next, stack the pages behind a construction paper copy of this cover and staple them together.

Quick Craft

Floating Along

Materials: 9" x 12" sheet of white construction paper, six 1" x 3" brown paper strips, blue watercolor paint, paintbrush, scissors, glue, crayons

Directions: Paint the bottom portion of the white paper so it resembles the ocean. Then color and cut out the pattern. When the paint is dry, glue the cutout to the paper so the tub looks like it is floating in the water. Next, glue the brown strips to the tub as shown. If desired, add other details.

TEC61259

Everything Nursery Rhymes • ©The Mailbox® Books • TEC61259

Fishing Fun

Color the pictures that end the same in each row.

ends like			
ends like			
ends like			
ends like			

Passing the Time

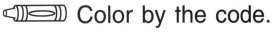 Color by the code.

Color Code

○ — yellow

△ — blue

□ — red

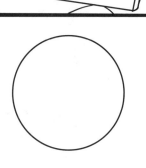

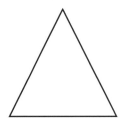

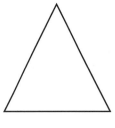
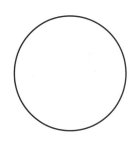
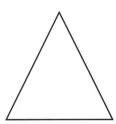
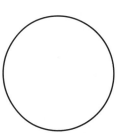

Name _____

Wavy Water

Draw 〰.

A New Ride

 Draw to connect the dots.

10
1

2

3

4

5

6

7

8

9

This Little Piggy

This little piggy went to market;
This little piggy stayed home.
This little piggy had roast beef;
This little piggy had none.
This little piggy cried, "Wee, wee, wee!"
All the way home.

Here's What Our Piggies Would Do!

Class Book Cover: Give each child a sheet of paper programmed with the prompt "If I had a pig, it would…" Encourage him to think of something his pig might do—such as ride a skateboard, take a bubble bath, or go to the movies—and then dictate or write a response and illustrate the page. Stack the pages behind a construction paper copy of this cover and staple them together.

Quick Craft

Market Piggy

Materials: small rectangle cut from a grocery bag, 1" x 6" pink construction paper strip, pink crayon, scissors, unsharpened pencil, glue

Directions: Color the pig pink and cut it out. To make the pig's curly tail, wrap the paper strip around the pencil and then slide the paper off. Glue one end of the tail in place. Then glue the rectangle to the pig's mouth so it looks like the pig is carrying a bag of groceries.

TEC61259

Playful Pig

Cut.

Glue to make matching letter pairs.

N		T
H		C
E		U

h u e t n c

u

c

Everything Nursery Rhymes • ©The Mailbox® Books • TEC61259

Peekaboo Piggies

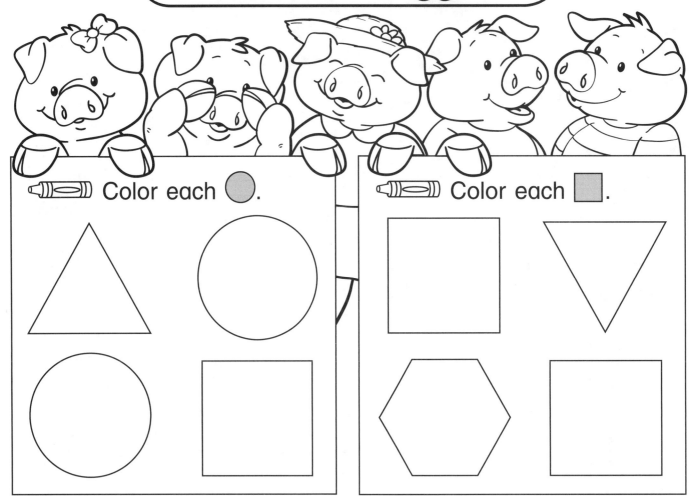

Color each ⬤.

Color each ▢.

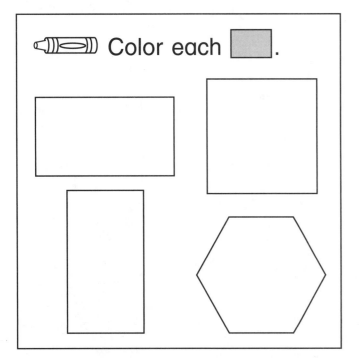

Color each ▬.

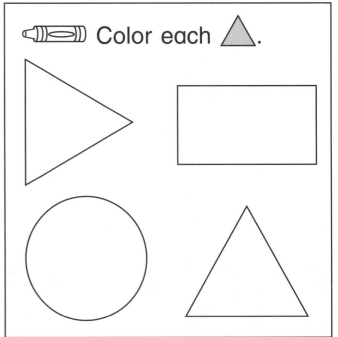

Color each ▲.

Everything Nursery Rhymes • ©The Mailbox® Books • TEC61259

Busy Little Pigs

Trace.

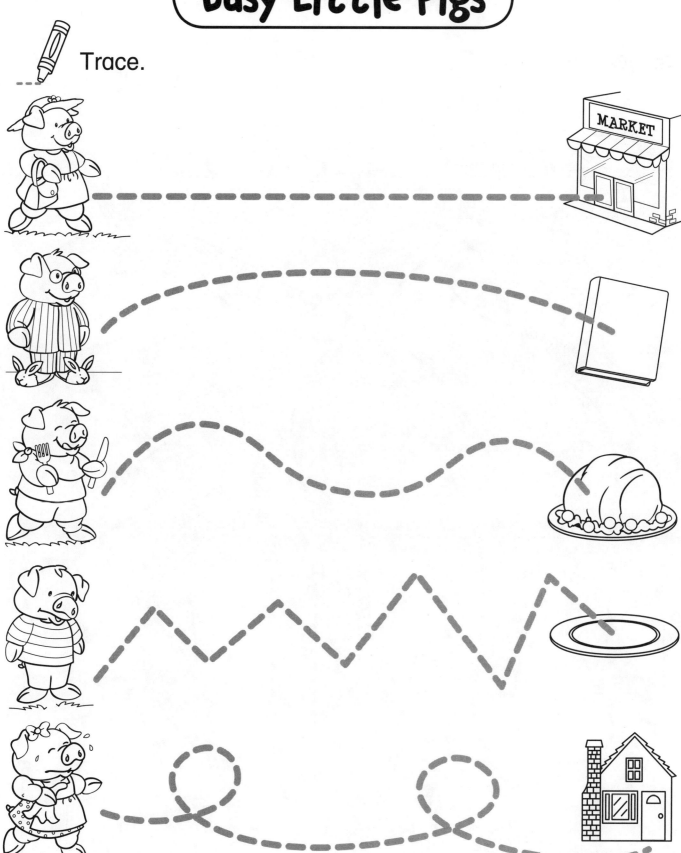

Name _____

Going to Market

Draw.

Help Pig find the market.

Everything Nursery Rhymes • ©The Mailbox® Books • TEC61259

Three Little Kittens

Three little kittens
Lost their mittens,
And they began to cry.
"Oh mother dear, we sadly fear
Our mittens we have lost!"

"You lost your mittens?
You naughty kittens!
Then you shall have no pie.
Meow, meow, meow, meow.
No, you shall have no pie."

The three little kittens
Found their mittens,
And they began to cry.
"Oh mother dear, see here, see here,
We have found our mittens."

"You found your mittens?
You good little kittens.
Then you shall have some pie.
Purr, purr, purr, purr.
Yes, you shall have some pie."

TEC61259

TEC61259

TEC61259

TEC61259

TEC61259

TEC61259

TEC61259

TEC61259

How to Not Lose Your Mittens

Class Book Cover: Give each child a sheet of paper programmed with the prompt "I will not lose my mittens because…" Encourage her to think of ways she could avoid losing her mittens, such as by putting them in her coat pocket, giving them to her dad, or making sure her dog can't take them. Then have her dictate or write a response and illustrate the page. Stack the pages behind a construction paper copy of this cover and staple them together.

Quick Craft

Freshly Baked Pie

Materials: 9" construction paper square, light brown tissue paper scraps, 1" x 5" aluminum foil strip, six 2" pieces of yarn, crayons, scissors, glue

Directions: Color the cat and her apron. Cut out the pattern and glue it to the construction paper square. Glue the aluminum foil strip (pie tin) to the rectangle. Crumple the tissue paper scraps (piecrust) and glue them above the pie tin. Glue three yarn pieces (whiskers) to each side of the cat's nose.

TEC61259

Name _____

Eating Pie

Color the rhyming pictures in each row.

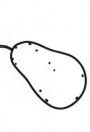

Name

Mittens, Mittens, Mittens Everywhere!

Listen and do.

Everything Nursery Rhymes • ©The Mailbox® Books • TEC61259

Note to the teacher: Lead students in following these directions. 1. Color the mitten that is *on* the chair. 2. Circle the mitten that is on the floor *between* the kittens. 3. Cross off the mitten that is *beside* the chair. 4. Draw dots on the mitten that is *above* the kittens. 5. Draw stripes on the mitten that is *under* the chair.

Name _____

Kitten's Mittens

Finish drawing the mittens.

Crumple.

Glue.

Everything Nursery Rhymes • ©The Mailbox® Books • TEC61259

Note to the teacher: After each student finishes drawing the mittens, have her crumple tissue paper and glue it to the page to fill in each cuff.

Where Are the Mittens?

Help the kittens find **6** mittens.

Circle.

Everything Nursery Rhymes • ©The Mailbox® Books • TEC61259

Twinkle, Twinkle, Little Star

Twinkle, twinkle, little star,
How I wonder what you are.
Up above the world so high,
Like a diamond in the sky.
Twinkle, twinkle, little star,
How I wonder what you are.

"Twinkle, Twinkle, Little Star" Picture Cards
Use the extra cards to make more "Twinkle, Twinkle, Little Star" rhymes.

TEC61259

TEC61259

TEC61259

TEC61259

TEC61259

Everything Nursery Rhymes • ©The Mailbox® Books • TEC61259

When I Look at the Stars...

Class Book Cover: On a sheet of paper, have a child draw what she sees when she looks at the night sky. Then have her dictate or write a sentence about her drawing. Finally, stack the pages behind a construction paper copy of this cover and staple them together.

Quick Craft

A Starry Mobile

Materials: 12" black tagboard strip, yellow-tinted glue, gold glitter, yarn, paintbrush, scissors, hole puncher

Directions: Brush yellow–tinted glue on the stars and then sprinkle gold glitter on the glue. When the glue is dry, cut out the stars and punch a hole in the top of each one. Then punch five holes in the tagboard strip and use a different length of yarn to tie each star to the strip. Punch a hole in the center of the tagboard strip and add a yarn loop for a hanger.

TEC61259

Name _____

Stargazing

Color by the code.

Color Code

1 part like — orange

2 parts like — yellow

Name_____

Counting Stars

Count.

 Glue to match the numbers to the sets.

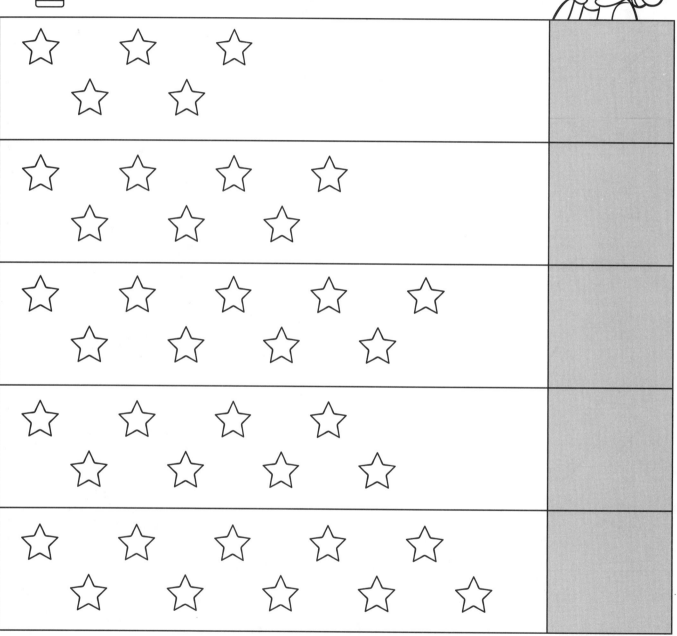

Everything Nursery Rhymes • ©The Mailbox® Books • TEC61259

7 8 5 9 10

Name _____

Under the Stars

Color.

Tear.

Glue.

Everything Nursery Rhymes • ©The Mailbox® Books • TEC61259

Note to the teacher: Have a child color the sky black and then color the rest of the picture as desired. Next, have him tear yellow construction paper scraps into small pieces and glue them to the sky so they look like stars.

Twinkling Star

 Cut.

Glue to make a picture.

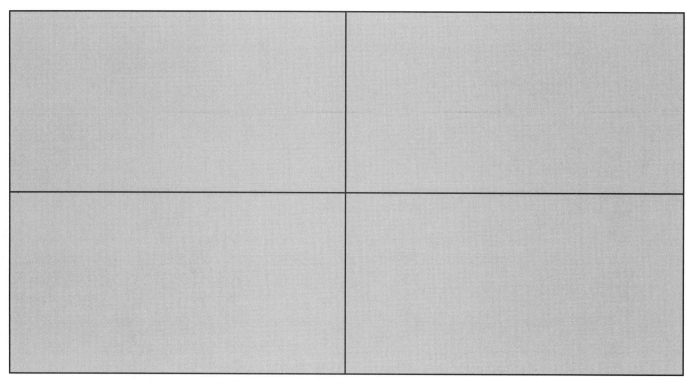

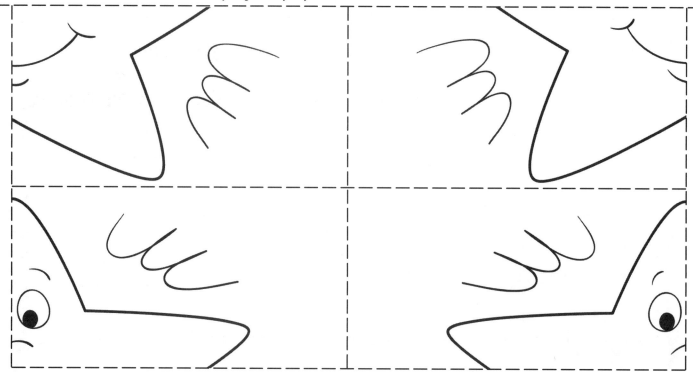

Nursery Rhyme Pals
A booklet-making activity

Materials for one booklet:
copy of pages 166–168
crayons
scissors
glue

To make a booklet:

1. Help a child write her name on the booklet cover on page 166; then ask her to color the pictures on pages 166–168.
2. Help her cut on the dotted lines on each page.
3. Read aloud the text on each booklet page. Help the child identify the missing picture and allow time for her to glue it in place.
4. Help the child cut out the booklet cover and pages. Then have her stack the pages behind the front cover.
5. Bind the booklet as desired.

A ____ jumps over the ____.

Nursery Rhyme Pals

Name _____

Everything Nursery Rhymes • ©The Mailbox® Books • TEC61259

A jumps over the 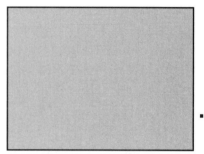 .

A loses its  .

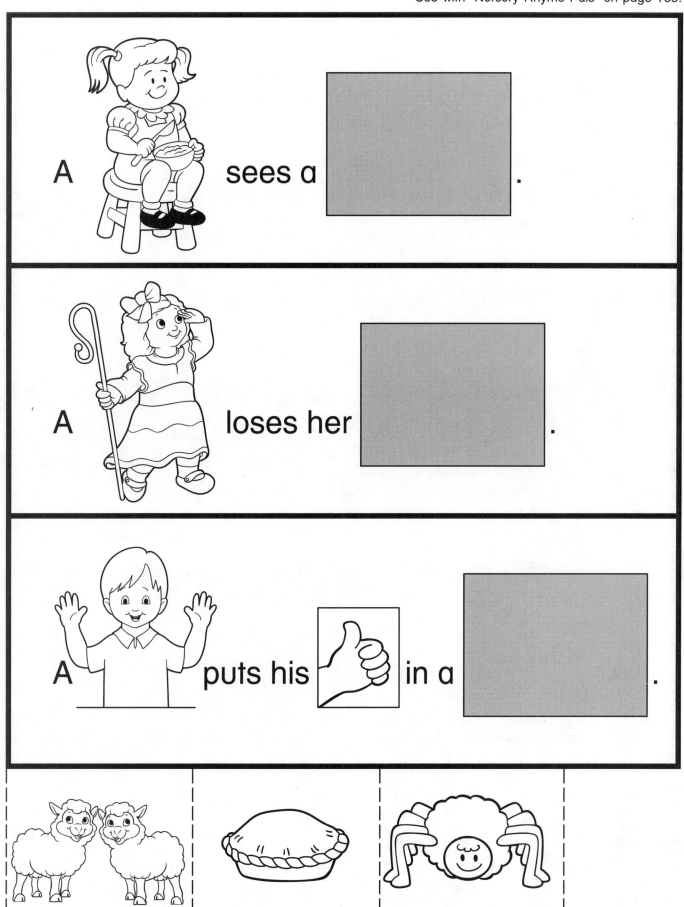

A [girl] sees a ▢.

A [shepherdess] loses her ▢.

A [boy] puts his [thumb] in a ▢.

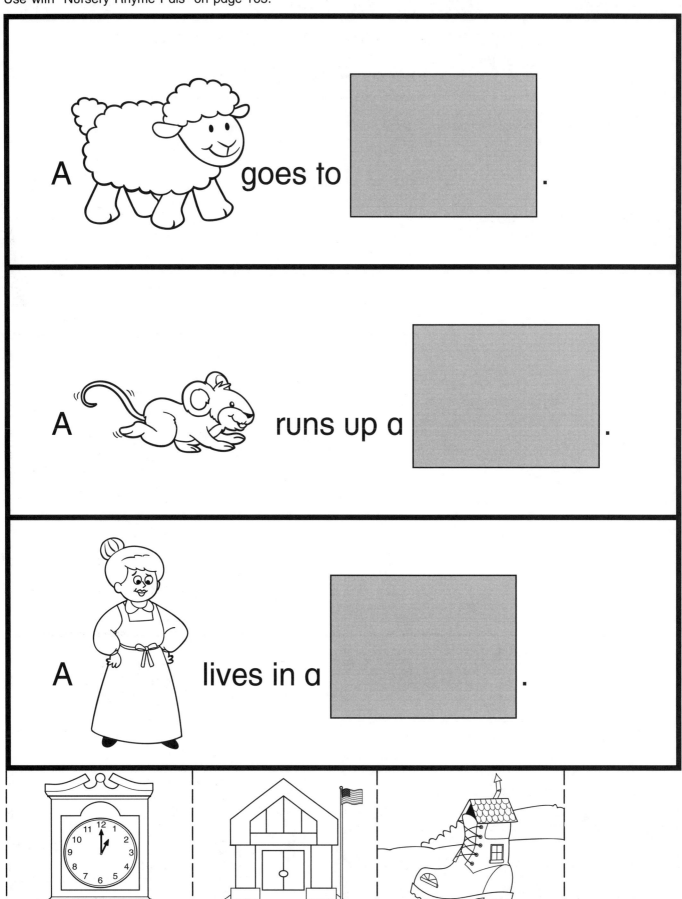

A ____ goes to ____.

A ____ runs up a ____.

A ____ lives in a ____.

Mother Goose Match
A memory game for individuals, partners, and groups

To prepare: Make two copies of the cards below and on pages 170 and 171. Cut out the cards. Next, select each card that shows an element from a nursery rhyme your students know. Find each card's match and shuffle the cards together.

To play: Lay the cards facedown. A player turns over two different cards. If the cards match, he removes them and stacks them nearby. If the cards do not match, he turns them over. Play continues until all the cards are matched. For a partner or group game, players take turns.

(For more ways to use the game cards, see the Bonus Activities on page 176.)

TEC61259

TEC61259

TEC61259

TEC61259

Game Cards
Use with "Mother Goose Match" on page 169.

TEC61259

TEC61259

TEC61259

TEC61259

TEC61259

TEC61259

TEC61259

TEC61259

TEC61259

TEC61259

TEC61259

TEC61259

Nursery Rhyme Cover Pattern

To make a cover, color and cut out a copy of the pattern. Glue the cutout to a 9" x 12" sheet of construction paper. Make a copy of each illustrated rhyme and bind the copies between the cover and a second sheet of construction paper.

TEC61259

Bonus Activities

Full-Page Illustrated Rhyme

Whole group: Cut a key illustration from copies of several rhymes. Place the illustrations in a bag. Have youngsters sit in a circle and pass the bag as you play soft music. Stop the music and direct the child holding the bag to remove an illustration and name the rhyme it is from. Then lead the group in reciting the rhyme. Continue until each illustration has been used. **Reciting a rhyme**

Center: Set out laminated copies of selected rhymes along with a set of letter cards and dry-erase markers. A child chooses a rhyme and a letter card. Each time the letter appears in the rhyme, he circles it. If the letter is not found in the rhyme, he chooses a different letter card. Then he counts the circled letters. If time permits, he chooses another letter card and repeats the activity. **Matching letters**

Jack and Jill went up the hill
To fetch a pail of water.
Jack fell down and broke his crown,
And Jill came tumbling after.

Ee

Bonus Activities

Picture Cards

Small group: For this sorting activity, gather two plastic hoops and cut apart a copy of picture cards for two different rhymes. Label the hoops with the corresponding rhymes' names. Then distribute the cards and invite each child, in turn, to place her card in the appropriate hoop. If desired, repeat this activity with other rhymes. **Sorting**

"Little Boy Blue"

"This Little Piggy"

Center: Color and cut apart copies of the picture cards for desired rhymes. Attach each card to a craft stick and place each set of the resulting puppets in a separate resealable plastic bag. Place the bags at a center. A child chooses a bag and uses the puppets to perform a nursery rhyme puppet show. **Oral language**

Everything Nursery Rhymes • ©The Mailbox® Books • TEC61259

Nursery Rhyme Pals

Individual: Program eight sheets of paper with a rebus sentence starter from the "Nursery Rhyme Pals" booklet. Make enough copies for each child to have one sheet. Give each student a sheet along with access to art supplies and magazines. Have him write or dictate the word that completes the sentence. Then have him draw or cut pictures from the magazines to illustrate the sentence. Invite him to share his completed project with his classmates. **Illustrating a sentence**

A [cat] loses its <u>mittens</u>.

Center: Make a sample "Nursery Rhyme Pals" booklet. Place the booklet at a center along with blank paper strips, pencils, and crayons. Using the sample booklet as a model, a child writes a different rebus sentence on each of several paper strips. He stacks the resulting pages behind a construction paper strip cover and staples them together. **Writing sentences**

Jake's Rhymes

A [spider] jumps over the [truck].

Mother Goose Match

Small group: Cut apart several copies of the game cards. Place one of each card in a small basket. Glue the remaining cards to tagboard rectangles, as shown, to make different lotto boards. Give each child a lotto board and six game markers. To begin play, take a card from the basket and recite part of the corresponding rhyme. Invite each student who has a picture from the rhyme on his board to cover it with a game marker. Then have a volunteer name the rhyme. Continue play until each child has covered his entire card and called out, "Mother Goose!"
Participating in a game

Whole group: Prepare game cubes by covering two small tissue boxes with paper. Then color and cut apart a copy of the game cards and attach one card to each side of a box. Invite a volunteer to choose a cube and roll it. Have her name the picture that is facing up and then help her lead the class in reciting the corresponding rhyme. **Oral language**